The Right to be Human

Biblical Studies in Human Rights

Chris Sugden
Director of Academic Affairs,
Oxford Centre for Mission Studies

GROVE BOOKS LIMITED
RIDLEY HALL RD CAMBRIDGE CB3 9HU

Contents

1. Introduction 3
2. The Right to be Human in the Old Testament 4
3. The Right to be Human Proclaimed by Jesus 9
4. God's Commitment to the Right to be Human:
   The Creation of a Community 18
5. The Right to be Human—How is it Shared? 22

Preface

These are essentially biblical studies, especially focusing on Isaiah 5, Matthew 23, Ephesians 1–2, Mark 10.35–45, Matthew 25.14-30 and Romans 8.18–39. They were originally given at the invitation of Dr Hunter Mabry of the United Theological College, Bangalore at a seminar on human rights held in the Whitefield Centre, Bangalore, India in 1981. They were published in an earlier version in *Religion and Society*, (the journal of the Christian Institute for the Study of Religion, Bangalore) vol XXIX, number 2, June 1982. The inspiration for addressing the issues of human rights by focusing on the right to be human, and much of the fundamental work in developing some of the biblical material here, owes much to my partnership with my senior colleague in India then, and Oxford now, Dr Vinay Samuel.

The issue of human rights is wider than the issue of rights before the law; the notion of human rights is under especial threat with the collapse of the enlightenment rationality which was the basis of the development of human rights in the West. The issue of the right to be human is also one of the four themes for the 1998 Lambeth Conference. So these studies are offered in an edited form as a contribution to the task of bringing the world we live in into the world of the Bible—to re-focus our eyes on the city that has foundations, whose builder and maker is God, where the right to be human will be fulfilled in all the glory God intended. I would specially like to pass them on to the three J's, who know who they are.

The Cover Illustration is by Peter Ashton

Copyright © Chris Sugden 1996

First Impression July 1996
ISSN 0951-2659
ISBN 1 85174 321 9

1
Introduction

It is especially important to address the issue of human rights in the context of Western academic discussion of the end of modernity. The collapse of enlightenment rationality and thus, in particular, many accepted arguments for objectivity put at risk claims to there being objective, mandatory rights for human beings.

In Christian thought, the foundation of human rights is in the gracious and unmerited love of God. God's love is revealed in Scripture as a love that bestows value on people. It is spontaneous and unmotivated. Grace cannot be understood as long as notions of the particular worth of the human object are entertained. God's love creates value. To speak of human worth always in relation to God will mean to restrict what is objectively valuable about our neighbour to what God has revealed in some distinctively authoritative act such as the life of Jesus.

The less that human equality is linked to observable human characteristics, and the less the religious state of affairs about human beings is held to be demonstrable, the more any definite evaluation of the rights and worth of human beings appears to be like a bestowal. Because God bestows worth on people, we ought to bestow worth on each other. We may share much in common with non-believers about human rights. But they will need radical adjustment in accord with the message of grace. So it is important to ground the value of the neighbour not in any immanent quality that he or she may possess, but as a status conferred by God. To seek justice is to enable people to have their place in a society in a way that expresses human dignity. To act in love is to affirm the grounds for such justice, the unmerited grace of God, and to act in such a way that each is accorded equal opportunity to experience such justice—to belong.

Human rights are rooted in a vision, a concept and a notion of what it is to be human. Being human cannot be reduced to or defined only in terms of human rights, as it embraces more than legal codes of rights. Human rights may be set down in legal codes, but people always have a tendency to by-pass them for ends which ultimately destroy human rights. Many historical illustrations come to mind where liberty has imprisoned equality and murdered fraternity. Yet the vision of the human must be protected in clearly defined rights. These must be set down in law. I wish to explore three theses in this regard:
- First, human rights are rooted in the larger right to be human;
- Second, the right to be human must be enshrined in human rights;
- Third, human rights are not sufficient to ensure the right to be human.

I will explore this in both Old and New Testaments.

2
The Right to be Human in the Old Testament

Human rights are clearly set down in the law of Moses. Scholars tell us that this law differed from other law codes of the time because it lay far greater emphasis on the value of human beings. From one perspective the law of Moses was the law for the settlement of the land of Israel. It enshrined the principles of earlier nomadic patriarchal communities.

Communities of Equality

One of the very important principles of the early nomadic patriarchal communities was equality. There was no social differentiation in the community. The whole tribe were rich or poor together, depending primarily on the yield of the pasture land. Private property was never used to oppress a neighbour or as a means to come by more property. Instead property was used generously to entertain guests and help the poor.

Due to this attitude and this use of wealth, wealth could never create social classes. The whole clan could be rich today and due to poor pastures or raids by enemies could be poor tomorrow. And this equality was closely related to the way the land and the resources available were shared. This principle was preserved in the law of Moses.

Land was divided up on the basis of the size and the need of each tribe, not on the basis of power, achievement or reward for services in battle. It was divided into equal portions according to the number of families in a tribe and was distributed by lot. The division was decided by representatives of each tribe who took part in the discussions, not by the strongest tribe. Once each family was assured in this way of its own inheritance, laws such as the Jubilee law prevented dispossession. The land belonged to Yahweh and so could never be alienated from the families to whom he gave it or from their descendants.

Not all the laws to prevent dispossession were fully observed. There is no evidence that the Jubilee law was actually observed in the historical period of Israel. But there is evidence that a basic equality prevailed in Israelite life, certainly up to the 10th century. By the 8th century there was a marked change. Rich houses were bigger and better built and in a different quarter from where the poor houses were huddled together.[1] Thus we have the situation described by Isaiah in his first woe or doom prophecy (5.8), 'You buy more houses and fields to add to those you already have. Soon there will be nowhere for anyone else to live, and you alone will live in the land.'

---

1 For further discussion see 'A Just and Responsible Lifestyle' by Vinay Samuel and Chris Sugden in Ronald Sider (ed), *Lifestyle in the Eighties* (Exeter: Paternoster, 1982).

Failure of Equality: Land as Commodity

A major change had come on Israelite society during the monarchy. This change can be traced to two particular influences. The first was that during the early monarchy the Israelites came into much closer contact with the Canaanites. They absorbed Canaanite cities into their state. They came into contact with Canaanite methods of social organization and the understanding of the land and resources that underlay it.

For the Canaanites land was a marketable commodity. Economic growth was the goal of their corporate activity. Through their fertility religions, the Canaanites sought to coax the fruits of the land to the maximum extent. The Israelites had no such fertility religions. Their law saw their land as a gift from God for whose use they were responsible and whose distribution was ordered by moral principles. God's blessings on the land depended on covenant faithfulness to God and justice among the people of God. Justice and humanity in the responsible use of the distribution of the land came before techniques to maximize profit.

In the Israelite model the equality and rights of each family was closely linked with the equitable distribution of land. In the Canaanite model this was not so. Rather, wealthy land owners lived in the cities and had their estates worked by slaves or by paid farm labourers. Commerce in the cities led to increased wealth which provided the means to provide more land in the countryside and therefore wealth tended to reinforce class divisions.

Failure of Equality: the Monarchy

The second factor that brought about social change was the institution of the monarchy. The Old Testament is ambiguous about monarchy. The warnings about the lifestyles of the kings in 1 Samuel 8.10-18 reflect contemporary Canaanite models of kingship. The goal of the kings in Israelite society was to maximize the economic affluence of their court and society. This was probably in response to the Canaanite models of kingship and to the need to compete favourably with other kings and prove their credentials. They put their duty to preserve people from exploitation a long second to their concern to prove that their kingship would bring economic affluence. The trade-off for economic affluence was inequality and injustice. So we find the following processes in Israelite society.

First, to maintain his soldiers and his court the king needed crown lands. Land which was vacated by families did not revert to the clan for re-allotment but fell to the crown who handed this out to royal officials in return for service.

Secondly, we find no evidence that the Jubilee legislation of the re-allocation of the land to its original owners was ever practised. That would have been very much against the king's interest.

Thirdly, Canaanite fertility gods were introduced into the Jerusalem temple.

Through alliances with local Canaanite rulers and other foreign rulers, foreign religions and deities were brought into the Jerusalem temple as a political move. This introduced a concept of God that was not rooted in justice and righteousness. It fundamentally altered the thrust of Israelite religion and worship by separating worship from the practice of righteousness and justice. For example, in Israelite worship one third of the offerings that were to be brought for thanksgiving for the fruits of the land were to be given to the poor and the widows (Deuteronomy 26.12-13). Isaiah 1.14-17 tells the Israelites that their worship disgusts God. Instead he wants them to see that justice is done for those who are oppressed, to give orphans their rights and defend widows.

Fourthly, the kings conscripted Israelite free peasants for labour. Israel had returned to Pharaoh's slavery.

Prosperity and Rights

All this was in sharp contrast to God's purpose that his people should be free and live with a measure of equality to be based on economic independence and rooted in an equitable share of the nation's wealth, resources and land. Every family had significance and a stake in the community because they owned land, ownership protected in law. The duty of the kings was to protect the rights of those whose land rights were infringed.

The continuance of this situation and the prosperity of the nation depended on faithfulness to the covenant not on correct fertility rituals. The rights of the citizens were bound up with the land and were to be protected by the king. Genesis 1-3 established the link between humanity and the land. People come from the dust. God gives them responsible dominion over the earth.

The kings undermined this interlocking edifice of society. Thus we come to the situation that Isaiah has to address in his doom prophecies in chapters 5 and 10. The wrongs Isaiah attacks assume the rights that people had under the covenant.

Woes and Blessings

The first set of woes are against the great landlords and the property owners (Isaiah 5.8-11). Land owners were buying up the land from the people and thus removing from people the basis of the legal security and their right to belong. Therefore their harvest will fail—not because of incorrect rituals, but because of unjust social relationships. The curses of the covenant in Deuteronomy 28 would come into effect. Isaiah affirms that there is no blessing on ownership or ownership of resources that is not morally justified. The Lord of humanity and of nature will see to that.

The second woe (verses 11-17) is against the nobility. Instead of exercising their responsibility on behalf of the whole nation and the common interest, the ruling class is only concerned with its own profit and pleasure. They begin drinking in the morning and continue well into the evening getting drunk.

The third woe is against the mockery of God's commands (verses 18-19). During economic prosperity unbelief became wide spread. People were indifferent to God's commands in their pursuit of extending personal power.

The fourth woe is against the perversion of God's truth (v 20). They call evil good and good evil. They turn darkness into light and light into darkness.

The fifth woe is against those who are wise in their own eyes (v 21). This ruling class were self-confident, clever and played the system to their own advantage very well. They were getting the maximum rewards out of their possessions.

The sixth woe is against impotent judges (verses 22-24). The people who were charged with administering the law were only concerned for their own profit and pleasure. Thus they became the tools of those who exercised power and authority and who handed them profits and pleasures on the condition that they turned a blind eye to the law. As a result the people who suffered were the poor, those whose land was removed without redress.

The seventh woe is in Isaiah 10.1-2, 'Woe to those who frame mischief by statute.' God's judgment rests on those who make laws to suit their own purposes. They promulgate laws that go against God's concerns in the covenant for the poor, or make government legislation which goes against the fundamental rights preserved in the constitution. They create a legal basis for the abuses described in the previous six woes.

The Appeal to Covenant

In all this Isaiah is attacking the undermining of human rights that are affirmed in the law of the land. He attacks business people who operate without conscience, rulers whose only goal is power and pleasure, and who have a cynical attitude to truth, morality and the rule of law. The basis of Isaiah's appeal is the God of the covenant, and the appeal to the covenant has a number of implications. First of all, God's character of justice and righteousness is central. God came to his vineyard and he expected to find justice and righteousness (v 7).

Secondly, the people's relationship with God is central. Israel is God's vineyard. God is not reducible to a principle of justice, or to a legal code. The covenant relationship with a transcendent God of justice is necessary in order to call the nation back to justice. The prophets were not primarily concerned to remind the people of legal precepts that were being overlooked. They stressed that people had a relationship with the God of justice and therefore if they are in that relationship they must live by justice.

Rights, Relationship and Grace

Thirdly, the mere reiteration of the law is not enough. Just to have the laws on the statute book is not enough to secure the right to be human. The law is continually circumvented by vested interests, and can only be re-established when people regain a relationship with the just and righteous law-giver. This relationship is not based on external allegiance only. The prophets looked forward to the day when the people would love the law and would obey it from the heart. And yet the law is not something that is internal alone. They also look forward to a new earth in which righteousness dwells, to a king who would judge the poor fairly and defend the rights of the helpless.

Fourthly, the covenant relationship affirms the right to be people, a right that affects the relationship between God and people, people and each other, people and resources and people and nature. God gives attention to whatever aspect of being human is being denied and ignored in the interests of the ruling party. He calls out his servants to proclaim that aspect at a particular time.

Fifthly, human rights are fundamentally rooted in the creative and redemptive love of God for every human being—in his grace, despite all our demerits, he loves each one as one and no more than one. Because God loves each person as one, he requires similar respect to be given by each human to all other humans. Human rights are thus not rooted in some intrinsic value of human beings, for some human beings would be perceived to lack it. Nor are they rooted in rationality or ability to communicate, nor in some contribution they have to make to others in a social contract, for again some would be perceived to be unable to make this contribution. In order to deny people human rights, it is first necessary to deny them the right to be human. If being human depends on some intrinsic worth or extrinsic contribution then it is always possible to exclude some people.

Thus human rights, to be applicable to all humans and not at risk of being manipulated or denied in the name of some larger interest, must be founded in the transcendent unmerited love of God.

Isaiah called the community of God's people to express justice, and to warn of judgment on injustice. The basis for both these calls was the covenant relationship with the transcendent God who loves justice—and calls us to practise it.

3
The Right to be Human Proclaimed by Jesus

Jesus' proclamation of the right to be human can be seen especially in his ministry to those kept outside the community of the people of God in Palestine. They had seriously diminished rights, and were socially disadvantaged for mainly religious and cultural reasons.

When Jewish cultural and national identity were under threat during the period of the Hellenistic rule, the Pharisaic party reacted against the Hellenization of Judaism by the Sadducees, who were the High Priests, the nobles, the most eminent citizens and leading men. They had made a political compromise with the Hellenistic overlords. They Hellenized Judaism.

The Pharisees' concern was to preserve their Jewish cultural religious heritage. They had learned thoroughly the lesson of the exile that God punished any infringement of the covenant law. Their hope for the deliverance of their nation from foreign rule was that God would bring the kingdom of God, God's promise in the prophets of a new heaven, a new land, a new earth, forgiveness of sins, and ultimately resurrection of the dead, to deliver his people—if all God's people kept all his law for one day. They sought to apply the oral traditions of the law and the rules for purity to lay people as well as to priests. They strictly observed all the traditions and detailed requirements of the law. They regarded all those who did not know the law or observe it as accursed (John 7.49), and denied them full civil and religious rights.

There was racial or caste discrimination. The only full Israelites were the pure-bred sons of Abraham. Pure ancestry had to be carefully proved for a man to be able to exercise any civic or religious rights, to share in the benefits accruing from the merit of Abraham, or in the messianic salvation. The Jews who lived in Galilee were tainted by intermarriage with Gentiles. Galilee was referred to as 'Galilee of the Gentiles.' Samaritans were outcastes because of their Jewish-Gentile origin.

Kingdom Equality

Jesus' challenge to discrimination was rooted in his proclamation and demonstration that the kingdom of God had already invaded history in his person. He announced that the kingdom of God had entered human history apart from Israel's obedience to the law. He undermined the Pharisaic conception of history, of what it was to be God's people and how God was going to deliver them.

The kingdom of God confirms and enables the right to be human. The kingdom of God transforms and redeems all humanity's relationships—the relationships between God and people, between people, and between humanity and the environment. On the basis of his proclamation and demonstration of the presence of the kingdom of God, Jesus challenged the discrimination exercised by the Pharisees.

Jesus specifically trained his disciples to reject caste discrimination in their community. First, most of his disciples were Galileans, the despised Jews. Jesus regarded himself to be from the same prophetic tradition as John the Baptist. He said that John had been preparing the way for him. John had specifically repudiated descent from Abraham as a sufficient guarantee of membership of God's people. Jesus held up Samaritans as examples of the love and gratitude which were required in the law. He refused to share the common hostility which even James and John showed. When passing through a Samaritan village which refused to recognize Jesus, James and John wanted to call down fire on that village, but Jesus refused (Luke 9.54). When Jesus found faith in a Gentile Roman centurion he said he had not found such faith even in Israel (Matt 8.10).

The early church continued Jesus' practice of refusing to recognize these racial barriers. After the death of Stephen, when the church of Jerusalem was persecuted and had to scatter, they fled to, and were welcomed in, Samaria. The Judaizers of course plagued Paul and the young church as they sought to make all Gentile converts conform to the Jewish law, but the council of Jerusalem in Acts 15 rejected this attempt to re-introduce discrimination into the fledgling Christian church. Paul, born a Hebrew of the Hebrews, stressed that in Christ there was no Jew or Greek. He clearly linked the breaking down of those barriers with the free grace with which God welcomes all people to his kingdom. Commenting on this Tom Houston says 'our roots and origins become secondary when God himself calls us to belong to his people. We all come in on the same basis, a gracious invitation from God, after we had already forfeited a thousand-fold any right to be included at all. This is the cure for class-consciousness, to by-pass the factors on which it is based and to start again on a new basis that treats everyone alike.'[2] Jesus started on the basis of the kingdom of God. He offered the invitation to the kingdom to all, and particularly to those who were excluded by the Israelite standards of racial and caste discrimination.

Men, Women and Rights

Second, sexual discrimination resulted from this Pharisaic interpretation of the law. In Jesus' time the Jews believed that sexual desire was uncontrollable. They set out to protect women and public morality by secluding women in private at home. Men could not trust other men with their women folk. Women suffered from this attitude. Because of men's inability to control their sexual desires women took no part in public life. They were preferably kept indoors. It was thought unfitting to address a woman in the street—even one's own wife.

---

[2] Address at Consultation on World Evangelization, Thailand, June 1980.

THE RIGHT TO BE HUMAN PROCLAIMED BY JESUS

Religiously, women were classed with Gentiles, slaves and children. They were allowed to listen to worship but not to take part in it. It was thought better to burn a copy of the Torah than to read it to a woman. Women were regarded as unreliable witnesses and could not give evidence in court. They had few rights in marriage. If a man committed adultery, it was a sin against the man whose wife he committed adultery with—adultery was a sin against another man, not against a woman.

But in the kingdom of God the lustful desires and the hardness of heart, which had been the cause of secluding women or divorcing them, were replaced by the quality of love by which men and women could relate as brothers and sisters in the community. Jesus only gave the hard teaching—that a man who looks on a woman to lust after her had already committed adultery with her—because the kingdom of God replaces wrong desires and hardness of heart with brotherly and sisterly love. Nowhere in the social sphere does the new life of God's kingdom make so striking an incursion into everyday life as with regard to women.[3]

Jesus showed that the blessing of God's kingdom were for women also by healing many women. He amazed his disciples by speaking in public with a Samaritan woman of an extremely dubious reputation. His teaching on divorce and adultery gave women a new status in marriage. He taught women religious truth. When Jesus said that Mary (rather than Martha) had chosen the better part—to sit at his feet and listen to his teaching—he was implying that it was quite right for Mary to listen to religious truth (Luke 10.42). Martha was a child of her age. She believed that Mary really belonged to the kitchen and was prohibited by law from sitting at the feet of Jesus listening to his teaching. Jesus did not agree.

A group of women accompanied Jesus and his disciples and cared for them as members of their community. Yet despite Jesus' moralizing on marriage, his concern for sexual purity and his condemnation of lust, we never find Jesus accused of immorality, even though he was a young bachelor moving around with a number of married women and former prostitutes ministering to him and other men. Women remained faithful to Jesus in moments of greatest danger when the men ran away. The women were the last at the cross and the first at the tomb. The resurrection narratives describe how Jesus first appeared to those most unreliable of witnesses whose testimony would be struck down in any court of law—women.

Traders and Children

Thirdly, there was occupational discrimination. A number of traders, shopkeepers and physicians were regarded as necessarily dishonest. Some trades

---

[3] Joachim Jeremias, *New Testament Theology* (SCM, 1971) p 227.

involved foul smells (the tanners). Others were suspected of immorality because they involved contact with women (tailors). Money-lenders and tax-collectors could never be judges or witnesses and were socially ostracized. Working people who had to engage in trade and mingle with Gentiles would not have time to tithe every piece of income or cleanse every vessel. Of necessity they were law-breakers in order to make a living.

Jesus himself engaged in trade as a carpenter. He ate with tax-collectors and those most immoral business people, prostitutes. He welcomed the tax-collector Matthew to his inner circle. Mary the converted prostitute was one of the women who travelled around with Jesus. To belong to Jesus' disciples meant joining a group which included people from the despised trades. When Peter went to Joppa he lodged at the house of one Simon, a tanner.

Fourthly, there was discrimination against children. Under Jewish religious law children were regarded as deaf, dumb and weak-minded. They were classed with Gentiles, slaves, women, the lame, the blind, the sick, the crippled and the old. Therefore it was quite natural for the disciples to scold those parents who brought their children for Jesus to bless. The disciples were children of their times as they implied that it was inappropriate and against Jewish law for the parents to try to bring the children to the teacher and scribe. But because of his proclamation that the kingdom had invaded Jesus brought children closer to God than adults. He said that a person could only enter the kingdom of God by becoming a child again. 'Do not forbid them to come because of such is the kingdom of heaven' (Matt 19.14)

Healing and Humanity

Fifthly, another group that was under social and religious taboo were the sick, the lepers and the demon-possessed. The healing that Jesus brought to these people was a foretaste and a first fruit of the resurrection and transformation that would come in the kingdom of God. The kingdom of God particularly brings healing to outsiders. Illness made you an outsider because you were thought to be suffering the righteous judgment of God, and would contaminate the community. Those Jesus healed were often double outsiders. They were not only ill but they were Gentiles (the Roman centurion's servant, Matt 8) or they were women (the woman with the issue of blood) or they were children (Jairus' daughter, Matt 9). And of course healing came also to the ultimate outsiders, the dead.

Jesus' healing broke the boundaries that men erected against these outsiders, the ill, the Gentiles, and the women. Jesus touched lepers and corpses. He healed the servant of the enemy centurion. And he welcomed these outsiders into his community. He restored the leper to the community and told him to show himself to the priest to show that he had been healed. He restored the dead son to his widowed mother as much so that his mother should no longer live alone as that he should live again. He called the woman with an issue of blood 'daughter' and made her stand out in front of the others to show that she was well. He restored Jairus' daughter, an outsider due to death, to her family.

Wholeness and Community

Jesus did not just heal people and leave them. He actually welcomed them into the community. In welcoming them in and in breaking the barriers he also redrew the boundaries. He commended the faith of the Roman centurion as an expression of faith that went far beyond any other expression of faith he had seen in Israel. Jesus was saying that the Roman centurion was in reality an insider. Those who had excluded him were the true outsiders.

Jesus was showing in his healing ministry that the coming of the Kingdom brings wholeness to the outsider whom society excludes. The Jews framed rules of ritual and religious purity to keep out the demon-possessed, the lepers, the women and the Gentiles. They prevented these outsiders touching anybody lest they pass on their contamination. Instead of the source of contamination contaminating him, Jesus embraced the contaminating person, and brought wholeness and cleansing. Jesus became an outsider himself. He was thrown outside on the cross. But he embraced their brokennesses, their contamination and their unwholeness and brought healing, wholeness and restoration.

Humanizing Law

In these five ways Jesus challenged the various forms of discrimination that the Jews had based on their understanding of the law and of what it was to be the people of God. Jesus took this debate with the Pharisees on the law beyond actions right into the nature of the law itself in Matthew 23.

The Pharisees sought to guard the Jewish heritage and identity by highlighting obedience to every jot and tittle of the law. Jesus' criticism was that they were selective in their obedience. They did what they could to obey God's law by focusing on provisions for religious rituals and worship. But in their social and economic context they were largely indifferent to Roman rule as long as it did not force them to break the Jewish law.

When Jesus encountered this practice of the law in Palestine he demonstrated that in his view the very purpose of the law had been subverted. For example, the observance of the Sabbath law was a badge of Jewish identity. Jesus attacked the Sabbath law on the grounds that it prevented people doing good to the sick and needy, for 'the Sabbath was made for humankind' (Mark 2.27). In Jesus' view the Jewish law had been subverted by being dehumanized. The law was dehumanized when petty tithing replaced the weightier matters of the law, justice, mercy and faith (Matthew 23.23); when in the interests of men's hardness of heart and uncontrollable sexual desire, women were kept secluded in private and could easily be divorced when it was considered necessary.

Interpretation and Context

Jesus criticized the Pharisees for dehumanizing the law by divorcing the interpretation of the law from the social, economic and political context in which it had originally been given and was meant to operate.

The law of Moses was meant to protect humanity and promote justice in the social context. The Pharisees, however, separated obedience to the law from the meaning of the law in its social context. In Matthew 23, Jesus' criticism was that because the Pharisees' interpreted the law in isolation from the social context, the law became an instrument to maintain the oppressive *status quo*. Those who suffered were the social and religious outcastes who were disadvantaged by various forms of discrimination. Therefore, instead of protecting the poor, the authorized interpreters of Moses' law 'tie on to people's backs loads that are heavy and hard to carry, yet they are not willing even to lift a finger to help them carry those loads' (Matt 23.4). The types of discrimination in Jewish society due to the interpretation of the law were the loads put on people's backs.

Instead of being servants the Pharisees wanted status, the best seats, to be greeted with respect and to be called teacher, father and leader. They had a very high status in Israelite society because people had to go to them to find out what they could and could not do. So they became masters. Jesus said that if they had read the law aright, the law would have made them servants.

The Pharisees locked the door of the kingdom of heaven in people's faces (v 13). They denied people the knowledge of God's law, which protected the women, the children and those who were now classed as outcastes. They also neglected to obey the really important teachings of the law. Jesus' key to understanding the law is 'justice, mercy and honesty.' But their concern for ritual cleanliness cannot hide their social oppression. 'You clean the outside of your cup and plate' (your religious concerns) 'while the inside is full of what you have obtained by violence and selfishness' (v 25).

Selective Obedience

Secondly, Jesus criticized the Pharisees because they so interpreted the law as to make it bearable to obey. The Pharisees selected those emphases in the law that they wished to obey—the religious requirements—and the context in which they were going to obey the law—the religious context. They developed highly sophisticated methods to wend their way through the demands of the law so that it became bearable for them. The Pharisees specifically avoided interpretation of the law that would involve a clash with the social, economic or political concerns of the Roman rulers.

Jesus points out that once the practice of the law designed in its original context to protect the poor is made bearable by the interpreters of the law for themselves, the poor lose the protection that the law affords. Life becomes more bearable for those at the top and more unbearable for those at the bottom. Their interpretation of the law was loading heavy burdens on to other people. Jesus declared himself on the side of the poor by calling all who were tired from carrying heavy loads and he would give them rest (Matt 11.28).

A similar understanding of the law underlies Jesus' encounter with the rich young ruler who declared that he had kept all the commands of the law. Jesus pointed out that his way of keeping the law in fact oppressed the poor. For he had obeyed a law subverted of its central concern of justice for the poor. Jesus called him to the concern when he asked him to give his possessions to the poor. If the ruler had really kept the true interpretations of the law, Jesus would not have had to make this challenge.

The Fulfillment of the Law

The most important response that Jesus made to the Pharisaic de-humanization and subversion of the law was that he was the fulfilment of the law. He fulfilled the law in two ways—by giving it its true meaning in his own life and by providing power to obey it. So though Jesus affirms human rights in the right to be human, his answer is not to rewrite human rights or even restate them. His answer is to say: I am the fulfilment of law, I give it its true meaning and provide the power to obey it.

Jesus fulfilled the law by giving its true meaning in context through the stances he took. By taking the side of the poor, eating with them and healing them he showed that the central concerns of the law were for the protection of the poor. The true interpretation of the law was not to be found in a new method of verbal interpretation of the Torah or in reworking the oral tradition. Following Jesus was synonymous with finding the fulfilment of the law. If Christ is torn from the context of the fulfilment of the law which God gave to promote justice and humanity, then such a Christ becomes a source of oppression. What the New Testament has to say about Christ and the law must be read against the background of Jesus' own stances in the social, economic, and political context. Jesus as the fulfilment of the law does not mean that the law is cancelled and we are justified by faith, but the law is fulfilled and is meant to be fulfilled in Christian obedience in following Jesus. Paul writes in Romans 8.4 that 'God sent his son so that the righteous demands of the law might be fully satisfied in us who live according to the spirit and not according to human nature.'

Life according to the spirit takes us to the second way in which Jesus fulfilled the law. Instead of reinterpreting the law to make it bearable, Jesus promised the experience of his power to those who pay the cost of following him in living out the full demands of the law. Jesus traced people's inability to face up to the true demands of the law for justice to their real motivations. These were revealed when people's behaviour and motivations were measured by the law's concern for justice.

Exposing the Motive

In Matthew 23, Jesus measured the Pharisees' behaviour and exposed their true motives for status and for maintaining their position of power. They lock the door and do not allow others to go in. They want to remain in charge and they give no one else the key to challenge them. Their motivations were greed and selfishness. Jesus pointed out that inhuman relationships are related to inhuman motivations, 'out of the heart.' He said to the Pharisees on a separate occasion that real defilement does not come from whether you wash your hands or not, but from out of the heart (Mark 7.19).

He knew the motivations that drove people. How could the people like the rich young ruler share the bias for the poor which the law taught, as long as the desire for riches ruled his heart? How could disciples relate to women as equals and sisters if lust rules in their hearts? How could James and John ever hope to serve if their ambition was for power and dominion?

Jesus taught that defilement came not from ritual impurity but from unjust social relationships which had their seat in people's motivations. If the law focused on ritual purity, people's motivations were not exposed because motive is irrelevant to ritual purity. As long as you engage in the process of washing your hands and cleansing the dishes, your motive is irrelevant. But once the law focuses on its central concern of justice in a context, especially for the poor, then key motivations are exposed. And Jesus promised that if people followed him as the fulfilment of the law, they would be joining a community which would enable to overcome lust, to renounce riches and to serve. Therefore this community would not need to follow the Pharisaic way of making the law bearable for themselves and avoiding its true challenges. They could take the yoke of the law upon them fully and find that, because Jesus was taking the yoke alongside them, they had the power to obey the law in its true concerns. Such a yoke was then easy.

To put this Nazareth manifesto into practice, Jesus knew of no other procedure than to follow, and serve, and commit one's life to the man from Nazareth.

4
God's Commitment to the Right to be Human: The Creation of a Community

Throughout Scripture, God's commitment to the right to be human is shown in his creation of a community that has structures for justice, forgiveness and reconciliation. This community had a clear role. It was called to be a light and a servant. The community was not just saved to be a particular people of God for its own benefit, and or to live for its own enjoyment. The right relationships that were established in their society were to mirror God's justice for the whole world.

Unfortunately this community often discredited God's commitment to it. The failure of the people of Israel to mirror justice discredited their God. God's commitment to the human shown in his creation of a community with structures for justice and forgiveness, was also shown in his exercise of judgment on that community when it failed. Judgment on injustice is part of God's commitment to the right to be human. There will never be a perfect community who live with perfect standards of righteousness in this world as it stands at present. The line between the human and the inhuman does not run between one community and another. It runs down the middle of each one of us.

Therefore provision was made for failure, for the community to receive God's judgment with grace. The law contained provisions for failure, for sacrifice to be made, for restitution to be given in cases where people had hurt or damaged other people's property, and for right relationships to be restored. If a master lay with a slave girl then provision was to be made for that girl to be married. There was provision also for forgiveness, and restoration between people and God.

Forgiveness and Failure

Yet in this community we find a continual cycle of cynical and persistent failure. Eventually God has to declare judgment without grace. He cancels his commitment to their land and drives the people into exile. Isaiah is given the vision that the way forward will no longer be an endless cycle of judgment and restoration. The way forward will be through a servant who would be the true Israel, who would be an individual and a corporate figure, an individual who leads a community (Isaiah 53). In the New Testament Jesus is presented as a servant who is able to create this obedient community. He will restore Israel to its true role as a servant and a light.

Jesus' goal in his ministry was to call Israel to repentance and to be the true people God wanted them to be—a true light and servant to the nations.

But Israel refused this call. So Jesus lamented: 'How many times have I wanted to put my arms around all your people just as a hen gathers her chicks under her wings. But you would not let me. And so your temple will be abandoned and empty' (Matt 23.37-8). Israel's persistent refusal of God's judgment and his offer of forgiveness for failure met finally with judgment without grace. The destruction of Jerusalem in AD 70 was God's vindication that Jesus had been his prophet.

The New Servant Community

Jesus formed a new community. He called them to be the true heirs of the promises to Abraham. The servant called the servant community around him. The doctor called the community of those who knew they were sick. Jesus applied many images of Israel in the Old Testament to his 12 disciples. They were to be the branches of him the vine, recalling the Old Testament picture of the vineyard. They were to be symbolic leaders of the new 12 tribes of Israel. In Ephesians the Gentiles are told that they are to be the fellow heirs. They now have a part in the covenants and the promises to God's people. They are built into a living temple unto the Lord. They are fellow citizens with God's people and members of the family of God. The New Testament letters focus on the life of the community together. The ethics that Paul commended in his letters are the ethics of the community. The ethical codes of the time presented the picture of the self-sufficient man of Aristotle or the heroic man of the Stoics. Paul's letters contained instructions for the growth of the community. The gifts and the ministries which will enable a body of people to grow are the gifts of each one which are given by God and should be developed and encouraged in order that the whole community can flourish. Everybody has a part to play.

God's commitment to the right to be human focuses on the centrality of the church, his people. This is not a narrow-minded sectarian self-concern. God's concern is to call and equip the servant community to be a light to the nations. The community is to be a home for wholeness, for a right understanding of what it is to be a human being. This community was to be God's instrument for achieving this in the world through its lifestyle, its witness, its proclamation and demonstration of the invading kingdom of God.

Kingdom, Church and World

The community was not to be God's only instrument in the world. The world in which he is at work is the world of humanity and of structures that express and shape people's relationships. In this world God is at work to bring his kingdom and to restore humanity. It is a world where many walls separate people from each other (Eph 2.14-15). That division that separated Jews and Gentiles was created by the structure of the interpretation of the Jewish law. How did God work in this world of humanity and its structures? 'The power working in us is the same as the mighty strength which God used when he raised Christ from death and seated him at his right hand in the heavenly world' (Eph 1.19).

The power of God is the power to bring life out of death, the power that raised Jesus from the dead. We cannot define God apart from Christ in the Scriptures. God's revelation reached its climax in the person of Jesus Christ. The means and pattern of God's work in the world is Christ's victory over sin, evil and death in his cross and resurrection.

In the New Testament God's power is always described as the power that brings life out of death. In Galatians it is described as the same power that enabled Sarah to conceive, to bring life out of death. Therefore we can look for the pattern of redemption and change at work in the world rooted in Christ, not necessarily tied to the instrumentality of the church. But wherever life is coming out of death in the world, wherever true redemption and change toward the pattern of justice and humanity that God has laid down is taking place, we can affirm that it is rooted in Christ, and is based on Christ's work, his death and resurrection.

The Sign of Restoration

What is the goal of God's work in the world beyond the church? The goal of all God's work (we read in Romans 8.19) is that all of creation waits with eager longing for God to reveal his sons. The restoration of the sons of God is God's purpose. The restoration of humanity, the crown of creation, is the key to the restoration of the whole universe. It was humanity's fall that precipitated the catastrophe that overtook the universe. The church is a sign that restoration is taking place. The church is the fellowship of those who are beginning to taste the experience of that restoration. God's work beyond the church patterned on the death and resurrection of Christ and enabled by that death and resurrection is to restore humanity and address and transform those structures which prevent the restoration of people to the fullness of life.

Barriers Broken Down

One major structure in the New Testament that was hindering the experience of the fullness of life and the right to be human was the Jewish-Gentile barrier caused by the interpretation of the Jewish law at that time. Wherever Paul went, he continually addressed this barrier, the structure which prevented true humanity, and true interdependence between people.

Therefore wherever change is taking place moving people towards the fullness of life, the pattern of being human, the wholeness of the restoration of humanity as shown in Christ, we can affirm it is related to Christ's death and resurrection. For only here were the ultimate barriers broken down and true inter-dependence and wholeness restored between the many parts of creation. In Gal 3.28, Paul writes that 'there is no difference between Jews and Gentiles, between slaves and free men, between men and women. You are all one in union with Christ Jesus.'

God is at work in the world beyond the Church to achieve his purposes of bringing back into wholeness and oneness the whole of humanity and all of creation. Humanity, instead of being split up into different groups, should be restored to wholeness and inter-dependence. This is in order to make possible the experience of fullness of life in Christ.

As people experience this coming together again, whether through the church or not, they experience a real blessing of the kingdom of God. That fullness of humanity is not possible if the Jewish-Gentile barrier continues, if men continue to dominate women and if the barrier between master and slave is continued. Therefore where we see these barriers being broken down in the world, we can affirm that it is God's work in Christ, moving people towards the experience of fullness in Christ, and opening them up to respond to him.

Incarnating the Right to be Human

In Christ is the fulfilment of the human. The fulfilment of God's commitment to the right to be human was that he became a human. The incarnation of the Word of God is the climax of God's commitment to the right to be human. And Christ is the image of God. The image of God is the one who perfectly does God's will. Christ is the true human being and is the head of a new humanity. He is the second Adam, the true Israel. Fullness of human life is experienced in the New Testament in union with Christ. We cannot be united with Christ on our own. We are in union with Christ. We belong to his body, the church, those who acknowledge him (Gal 3.26-28; Eph 2.15-18).

Christ is the fulfilment of the right to be human and in union with him is the experience of the fullness of humanity. If we do not relate to the body of Christ, the church, we are not related fully to Christ. We find this concern for community in Jesus' own ministry. Jesus himself called the disciples to be with him. Jesus does not start his work and then say to his disciples, 'Let me finish my work and then you can start yours.' Jesus calls the disciples from the very beginning of his ministry to come with him, to be with him, to be involved with him, to take the stance he takes, and to suffer the insults and the rejection that he suffers.

Then when he had gone away, he grants them his Spirit. The book of Acts shows that the work of Jesus continues because his Spirit is with those whom he called to be his community. So God's work throughout the world of people and the structures which form it is based on the work of Christ. It is focused on the community of his people. The community of his people is an instrument of God, and his kingdom, even though it is not the only one. Yet the community of the people is the goal of all God's work. As people come near to Christ and are opened up to Christ in many ways, the experience of the fullness of life in Christ is linked with membership of the community of the body of Christ.

Finally, what is the relationship between the Christian community and other communities? A community is based on shared values. Members often live in a common context but not necessarily so, and certainly hold a common world view. The Christian understanding is that Christ shows the values of the true human. These values would include loyalty to the whole human community, the uniqueness of the individual, compassion, forgiveness, servanthood, sharing, equality, justice and peace-making

The calling of the church is to image these values as it is conformed to the image of Christ. It is to live out these values, to address the values of the various wider communities in which she finds herself, to move the whole community towards Christ, and to express and experience the values of his humanity.

6
The Right to be Human—How is it Shared?

Legislation is important for establishing human rights. But we must do more than promote legislation if legislation itself is not to come into disrepute. We must share the life of Christ the true human, if we want to promote the right to be human.

The climax of sharing of the right to be human is seen in the incarnation. The incarnation is the climax of God's affirmation and commitment to the right to be human. God became human that we might become human. Jesus said: 'I have come that you may have life—life in all its fullness' (John 10.10).

Incarnation is the climax of God's communication with humanity (Heb 1.1; John 1.14). Jesus was not an illustration of truth that could be arrived at from other grounds. He was not a principle which was then applied in a particular situation. The meaning of the Word of God was not fully known until he became flesh in the actual situations of Palestine in the first century AD.

Jesus is neither an analogy, a parable, nor an illustration of the word of God. He is the Word of God become flesh and we do not fully know His meaning until we encounter the word in flesh.

Neither did Jesus become a universal human. He did not become a cipher or a symbol of man. He came as a real man with all the cultural, economic, social, personal and religious heritage of the Jews. He came as a Jew to the Jews. He came as a specific person, as a carpenter born in a poor family to a specific situation.

Incarnation and Context

From this we discover, first, that incarnation takes the context seriously. Jesus entered the real problems, debates, struggles and conflicts of the Jewish people, for instance debate about what it meant to be God's people and what obedience to God required in the light of the Gentile occupation of their Holy land. Jesus entered into this debate. He clashed with the Pharisees and Sadducees about how to be obedient to God. He took the side of those who had no voice in this debate, those who suffered discrimination through the operation of the current interpretation of the Jewish law. God's word was made known to Israel, as he became involved in the context.

Secondly, incarnation takes the audience seriously. Jesus did not address people impersonally, with universal truths which were applicable to anyone. He did not treat the Jews as ciphers, as token representatives to receive truths that were in fact directed at everybody.

Jesus came to his own. He spoke in terms that directly applied to the Jews.

He claimed to be fulfilling the mission of the Jewish messiah in Luke 4. He challenged the position of Moses in interpreting the law. He broke the Jewish laws of the Sabbath and the food laws. He even told Gentiles that he was sent primarily to the Jews first and that any benefits that accrued to them from his ministry were an 'extra.' Jesus' whole person, his being a Jew, his actions and his attitudes were set in a specific Jewish context. He was taking his hearers seriously in their context with their problems, their hopes and aspirations.

Thirdly, it may look as though incarnation removes Jesus from our context. However, on deeper inspection his incarnation brings him closer to us. Jesus addressed his total context in its religious personal, social, economic and political forms in its own terms by becoming incarnate. Judaism like Hinduism and Islam is a culture religion, an all-embracing total view of reality. Jesus communicated a critical and transforming word about the right to be human to that culture religion through being incarnate in the context. The scandal of particularity of the incarnation enables him to address each particular situation in our world.

Fourthly, Jesus became involved in the context and took stances in the context. The resources and the basis for his criticism and transformation of society came from outside. He was God's Word, the agent and expression of the kingdom of God. His mission was to bring the invasion of the kingdom of God, to bring God's word to the society. Incarnation does not remain outside. It comes inside and becomes concrete.

Communicating Change

Fifthly, Jesus gives us the pattern that the way to communicate the right to be human is not to act in general terms, but to become specific in each situation. John's gospel is often thought to be the most 'other-worldly' gospel. But in John's gospel Jesus talks about the water of life as he asks a drink in public of a Samaritan woman who is a lady of dubious morals. He breaks the law which forbade men to talk with a woman in public as he crossed that Jewish/Samaritan barrier. He talks about being the light of the world as he heals a man born blind, supposedly suffering because of his sins or his parents' sins. In a way that affirmed their humanness he communicated that the source of that humanness lay beyond the merely human.

Sixthly, incarnation stands on the side of the poor and for justice, making the word of God meaningful and real in the situation and bringing resources from outside to change the situation, providing a basis for continuity and change. There is continuity in Jesus' incarnation. He became a Jew. He fulfilled the hopes and aspirations of the Jews. He spoke in the terms of their longed-for deliverance. And yet there was change. Jesus transformed Judaism. He was a true Jew, the true Israel, and yet different from any of them. He fulfilled the promises to Abraham—continuity. He changed the nature of the fulfilment—change.

Seventhly, incarnation gives meaning. The incarnation was where the word gave its meaning by becoming flesh. Incarnation provides the model for our interpretation of God's word. As we become flesh ourselves, as we incarnate the Word of God, so we communicate its meaning to the world around us.

The Servant Model

These seven ways of incarnation give a model for how to share the right to be human. A very important aspect of Jesus' incarnation leads us further. Jesus became incarnate as a servant. Philippians 2 describes how Jesus did not count equality a thing to be grasped, but of his own free will gave up all he had and took the nature of a servant. (Phil 2.7-9). Paul sees incarnation in terms of servanthood. He uses this hymn as an argument to the Philippian Christians that they should not be seeking their own selfish interests but they should have the mind of Christ in them and should seek the interests of others (2.4-5).

To seek the interests of others is the role of a servant. A servant, when she comes into a home in India, or into the grounds of an institution, is there to do the bidding of those who run the place and to seek the interests of others. That is what Jesus did when he came into our world, and what we have to do as we are sent into the world.

Jesus himself understood his incarnation as servanthood in Mark 10.44-45. When James and John asked him for guaranteed seats at his right hand and his left when he came into his kingdom, Jesus contrasted the authority and power which was exercised in the world with that which was to be exercised in the kingdom.

Jesus contrasts his stance of servanthood with the power that was exercised over people. The rulers of the heathen have power over them. Power over people tends to use people as extensions of oneself, reduces, demeans and dehumanizes them. It treats people as objects in one's own task. The power that builds up people comes from underneath and is the power of servanthood. The servant has no agenda of his or her own, and has no status to defend. The servant is free to enable others to develop. The servant is not threatened by the initiatives or the gifts of others. Power that enables people to become subjects, to take initiatives and to develop all their potential, is the power of servanthood.

The Power of Servanthood

This power of servanthood was institutionalized in the early church in the doctrine of the gifts and ministries—every member, no matter how insignificant, had a vital service to give to the life of the whole community, a vital contribution to make, and a vital talent to develop. The development of the whole body depended on the gifts and the contributions of each one. If one member was not able to contribute or to play a role then the whole body suffered, was the weaker and the more impoverished. If any part of society is not able to function or contribute or grow in humanness, the whole body politic is impoverished. The only people who want to stifle initiatives and gifts in others and stifle the development of every member are those who seek to exercise complete control of dominating power.

In talking about this form of power, Jesus challenged Roman power which was based on the view that the strong should use their force and wealth to enrich themselves and to subjugate others. Jesus rejected the concept of power based on using one's strength to one's own advantage. He rode on a donkey into Jerusalem in direct contrast to the Roman commanders who entered with horses and chariots.

He undermined the basis of Roman power by advocating substantially different social patterns. He built a community out of those without power in society. He trained them in different ways of exercising power. They were not to retaliate when violent power was used against them. Jesus demonstrated that power was released when the victims accepted suffering. Jesus taught his disciples to carry the cross. They were not to exercise leadership by domination but by service. Leadership was open and gave power to everyone who would serve. Instead of approaching the Romans to use their power to achieve his ends, Jesus sent his disciples to the victims of Roman power exercised in domination.

He himself identified with the victims of such power by living in 'Galilee of the Gentiles,' as an artisan who had to pay Roman taxes. He spent his time with the poor and outcastes. And he died as a result of the collusion of the Sadducees, Pharisees and Romans on the Roman's instrument of torture. He called his disciples to go to the victims in the same way, and to be prepared to suffer the victims' death of the cross. As the disciples lived a community life and engaged in mission in this way, they would receive the power from the one to whom all authority and power in heaven and earth was given.

The Book of Acts describes how, when this power was released, the early church was able to do what neither Roman military might nor Jewish legalism could achieve. That was to bring together Jews and Gentiles, slaves and free, men and women into a new community of love and trust and mutual service. Jesus' servanthood pointed the way to a social order where neither the Romans nor any oppressing group could hold sway.

Oppressors hold sway because there are those who are willing to tie themselves to their coat-tails and kiss their feet to gain an advantage. But if service is the hallmark of each member of a community, there is no way in which oppressors can arise or rule.

Differentiated Stewardship

Servanthood is shown as the means of incarnation in the parable of the talents (Matthew 25.14-30). The king calls his servants and gives them 10 talents, 5 talents and 1 talent. No redistribution takes place after the master has given out the talents. Jesus is not legislating for a levelling down of all. He is not asking that the doctor or the university teacher become the same as the sweeper. Nor is the reward given on the basis of the increase made. The person who made the 10 talents more did not keep them. He was given greater responsibility and the extra talents given to the master. The use we make of our resources does not entitle us to keep the resources we gain. We are given talents to exercise in stewardship for the good of the whole body.

Servanthood is not defined here in terms of levelling everybody down to the same common denominator, denying the differences between people. Nor is it that as each develops his talents and resources for himself some unseen hand of the market by a sort of alchemy turns individual selfishness into communal benefit. Servanthood is to make use of all one's resources for the master's purpose of enabling the humanization and the fulfilment of others, especially the poor. The equality envisioned in servanthood is that all should equally abdicate their rights and become servants of each other to enable the fulfilment of all.

The Mandate of Servanthood

Incarnation and servanthood are Jesus' mandate for the church (John 20.21 and John 13.14). The Christian community should see its identity and distinctiveness not in its power but in its ability to serve, not in holding on to a place of security and respect but in giving its life away, not in maintaining position but in giving it away. Jesus taught in Mark 8 that we find our life by losing it. Paul wrote to the Corinthian Christians that the pattern of ministry is to be the pattern of death and resurrection of Christ (2 Cor 4.10-12). Death and resurrection should be the pattern of Christian ministry because it was the pattern of Jesus' ministry. Such death and resurrection is not natural to us. We naturally want to preserve ourselves and survive. But the pattern of death and resurrection is motivated by Jesus' own death and resurrection. The way of the cross teaches us the way to life is to give life away.

Futurologists predict increasing conflict between different interest groups fighting for their own share in the scarce resources, each under the slogan of social justice. Within this context the church as a servant community that seeks the interests of others, that gives its life away and that seeks the fulfilment of all will have a vital role to play.

Victory over Powers of Evil

How can we enable others to be servants when we know our own inadequacies? The flaw in our world is deeper than the problem of personal failure or inadequacies. The Bible describes demonic powers of evil which possess persons and pervade structures, societies and the created order.

So deeply flawed is our world that the Bible asserts that the whole creation itself must be restored in order that the right to be human might be fully restored. (Romans 8.19-22) This deep flaw in creation is not a cause for depression, frustration or inactivity, because the victory of Jesus that we celebrate is a victory that is all embracing. The method of the achievement of the victory was all-embracing. Jesus died because he identified politically with the outcaste groups and he suffered their fate. Jesus died because he was rejected by God's people who were expressing their rejection of God himself. He was wounded by their transgressions. And Jesus rose in a total physical transformation of his body to a completely new level of existence.

The restoration encompasses the evil powers. We celebrate the defeat of evil powers. We celebrate that the strong man has been bound and the captives are being freed. (Luke 11.21)

The victory embraces the sphere of persons. On the cross, God loved his enemies so much that he died for them to turn them into his friends and servants. Their accounts have been cleared, their debts paid, and their forgiveness assured. Jesus' death is spoken of in the New Testament as the death of the suffering servant. He was wounded by the transgressions of the people of Israel, and for their transgressions.

The victory also covers the sphere of the physical. At the last supper Jesus celebrated his victory in a feast and looked forward to the final feast in the kingdom of God. The gospels tell us the feast of the kingdom of God is especially for the poor, the crippled, the lame, the blind and those in the roads and lanes, the outcastes and the Gentiles. It is a feast to which the weary and heavy-laden, those oppressed by the interpretation of the law, are specially invited. It is a feast for those who identify with the powerless in their attitude to God, who take the attitude of not trusting in themselves but trusting in God.

The first fruits of this victory are now being experienced As Paul says 'we who ourselves experience the first fruits of the Spirit groan for the final consummation' (Rom 8.23). Our very frustration is an evidence of the first fruits of the Spirit because we know God has got something greater. God's purpose cannot be fulfilled in this world as it stands. It needs a total change. And yet we do experience the first fruits of the spirit. Hendrick Berkhof writes about Christ's reign and victory in the present:

> 'The Lord who makes his entrance into the world through the missionary proclamation is the Redeemer who comes to seek and to save what is lost. A new idea of being human is ushered in; it is not the proud humanity of the Greeks, but the humanity of humility. The battle is pitted against exploitation, injustice and slavery and against everything which is not motivated by love. The idea of social justice so well known to us was injected by the missionary proclamation.'[4]

Sexuality and marriage cease to be semi-fertility rites and now become personal

---

[4] Hendrik Berkhof, *Christ the Meaning of History* (John Knox Press, 1966) pp 88-89.

encounters. The state loses supremacy for we must obey God rather than people. Nature loses its divine status to be dominated and subdued by humanity. It is a resource to be shared rather than a divinity to be coaxed. It is plastic to technology and labour. The world receives a value. The world and its people are basically one, made by one creator and to find their goal in unity. Caste, race, tribe, sex and employment are to be aspects of that unity in diversity, not barriers between inferior and superior groups.

The changes that the kingdom brings always have the possibility of the demonic if they are not related to Christ. Science gave us both medicine to wipe out disease and the nuclear bomb to wipe out the human race. The coming of the kingdom unleashes both the power of God and the resistance of evil where Satan sees his goods being despoiled.

But our hope is based not on our perception of the first fruits. Our hope is based in the victory already won. (Romans 8.24-25). Our struggle is based on hope. We enter the struggle because we are certain of the final victory, because Christ has won it. The struggle is not just to be entered on the levels of organization and strategy. Prayer enters the struggle at a very deep level. Suffering also has a very important role in the struggle. In Christ our sufferings are redemptive.

Paul assures us that nothing we encounter in the struggle can separate us from the love of God through Christ our Lord (Rom 8.39). The love of God through Christ which won the victory on the cross and the resurrection is the basis and guarantee of the right to be human; it has restored the right to be human; and it is the foundation of our certainty that one day, when Christ returns, the right to be human will be displayed in all its fullness and enjoyed in all its richness. It is on the basis of that certainty that we enter the struggle to enjoy the first fruits of victory now, and to share them with the whole of God's creation.